I've known Bernie De Souza for over
for teaching people specific skill sets fills his diary as a speaker, trainer, and coach. He can teach you to do the same! We totally believe in Bernie's methods. That is why over 2,000 of our Personality Insights, Inc. Consultants are encouraged to listen when he teaches. Now you have his methods of getting more bookings in writing. Study them well and watch what happens to your business.

—Dr. Robert A. Rohm, PersonalityInsights.com

Mark Davis has two passions in life: traveling and speaking. From Russia to Brazil, from Hungary to Japan, from Australia to Chicago, Mark accepts speaking invitations only to destinations he wants to visit. He gets paid for his passion to speak, and knows how to get the bookings to create the life of his dreams.

—Jonathan Yap, author of *The Essential Handbook of Prospecting for Network Marketers.*

I like the hardcore, step-by-step, "how-to" approach that Tom "Big Al" Schreiter uses in marketing. No time wasted. We get to the problem. Then, we fix it right away with proven methods that work in real life. No theories. No generic preaching. Just what to do to get immediate results.

—Wayne Sutton, DoneForYouCoaching.com

How Speakers, Trainers, and Coaches Get More Bookings

12 Ways to Flood Our Calendars with Paid Events

BERNIE DE SOUZA, MARK DAVIS, AND TOM "BIG AL" SCHREITER

How Speaker, Trainers, and Coaches Get More Bookings

© 2020 by Bernie De Souza, Mark Davis, Tom "Big Al" Schreiter

Published by Fortune Network Publishing

PO Box 890084

Houston, TX 77289 USA

Telephone: +1 (281) 280-9800

BigAlBooks.com

ISBN-13: 978-1-948197-65-6

CONTENTS

PREFACE

Want to be a public speaker, trainer or coach?

Why not? It is a fulfilling, high-paying profession.

Oh … but there is a problem.

Most speakers are great speakers, but terrible marketers. No matter how well we speak, we still need an audience.

Most initial marketing attempts are:

- Hoping.

- Wishing.

- Begging.

- Posturing.

- Pretending.

- Brochure-making.

- Cool business cards.

- Emails.

- Cold calls.

Let's face it. It just looks bad when we have to sell ourselves as a speaker.

"Hi. I speak really well. Want to hire me?"

There is so much wrong with this.

But if we don't market, promote, and sell our speaking services, no one else will.

Anyone can be an unemployed speaker, hoping for the phone to ring with a speaking offer. That is not a career. That is bankruptcy.

Instead, let's do this. We can fill our calendars with high-paying speaking, coaching, and training events.

And to do this? We only have to become better marketers than our non-marketing competition. Fortunately, that isn't hard.

Do we have to fill every day with speaking, coaching and training?

Well, Bernie does. Bernie books himself five days a week, 45 weeks a year. Every year. Now, we don't have to be as busy as Bernie, but most speakers would love to speak more frequently. And coaches and trainers want to fill their diaries.

Want to fill your diary with clients? This book is for you.

Please note the following disclaimers:

- Throughout this book we will talk about speakers. But these techniques apply to trainers and coaches. It would be tedious if we had to say, "speakers, trainers, and coaches" every time.

- These are just some of the ways the three of us get our bookings. Will every way work for you? No. You might choose which ones fit your personality or business model. And your version might be better or worse (hopefully better).

- Pick the ways you will enjoy. One of the keys to happiness is to enjoy not only what we do, but how we do it.

So for all the trainers, coaches, and speakers, grab your pens and paper and take notes.

What this book is not.

We assume you already know how to speak, train, and coach.

If you are looking for tips on how to perform better in your profession, this is not your book. There are plenty of books and courses on how to be a better presenter.

If you are looking for strategies on how to close from the front of the room, get higher revenues per attendee, create products to sell, or to have more interesting openings to your talks, this is not your book.

We will add a few resources in the back of the book for these things.

This book only concentrates on getting more bookings and clients.

That is it.

Let's get started.

"Once upon a time ..."

"Once upon a time, a young man dreamed of becoming a public speaker. He won Toastmasters' competitions. Had walls of ribbons and awards. Studied his message thoroughly. Took advanced courses and coaching certifications.

"He posted his dreams and qualifications on his social media channels and received likes and favorites. He felt great that he was on his way to being heard.

"He dreamed of delivering his message to others. And he dreamed, dreamed, and dreamed. After many good nights of sleep with wonderful dreams, he woke up one morning, and he was old. And broke. No one ever heard his message."

Kids need to eat.

When no one is booking us, we have to motivate ourselves to create our own events.

Bernie invited local entrepreneurs and small business owners to his evening marketing workshops. His audience learned basic sales and marketing skills for their trades or small businesses. At the end of the workshop, Bernie offered his services to create a website, a video for the website, and some advertising copy.

What could go wrong?

- Renting a meeting room only for nobody to show up.
- Entrepreneurs canceling their appointments for Bernie's videographer.
- Rising early every morning to attend breakfast networking events to find more prospects.
- Producing the videos and websites.

But, kids need to eat. Bernie's family expected food and shelter.

And then it happened. At one networking event, an attendee gave Bernie a phone number. A company wanted better sales and phone skills for its salespeople. That was Bernie's expertise.

One phone call, one workshop booked.

Then, Bernie used the best marketing strategy ever. He delivered exactly what the audience needed. Great word-for-word skills of exactly what to say, and exactly what to do.

Bernie's performance went viral. Not because of his speaking skills or charisma, but because he delivered content that was exactly what the audience needed. An entire industry embraced Bernie not only in his own country, but internationally as well.

One workshop. One great delivery of exactly what the audience needed.

Solve the fear.

Does Mark love to speak? That would be an understatement. He lives to speak.

How does 17 cities in 19 days sound to us? Maybe awesome. Or, way too much. But for Mark, traveling from his home country of Australia to the United States, and conducting 17 public speaking workshops in 19 days, felt great.

How did this happen?

Mark worked with two direct selling publications with subscribers in the United States. The publications offered a chance for their "shy" subscribers to overcome their fear of public speaking by attending a three-hour workshop. All Mark had to do was show up.

And, of course, this led to future business and bookings. The attendees loved the workshops. Some asked Mark to stay longer and talk to their companies.

When people have a fear or problem to solve, it won't take much to get them to commit to workshops.

Free international travel?

For Tom, he wasn't a public speaker. Yes, he did small training workshops, but no keynote speaking or large group events.

40+ years ago, he wrote a book that included some of the skills he taught. And then Tom got this phone call from Hong Kong. Here is the short version.

"Hello. Are you the expert author of this book? Please come to Hong Kong and speak at our convention. How much do you charge?"

He thought, "Hong Kong? I have never been to Hong Kong. That would be a fun trip, sort of a mini-holiday. My wife loves shopping. I could take her."

Tom told the caller he would come if the caller would put them up in a hotel and pay their airfare. The caller loved the offer. Tom's wife was ecstatic.

They stayed the week while his wife worked full-time to support the Hong Kong economy. It was one of the best holidays ever. While in Hong Kong, Tom did two more paid workshops for the group.

He was hooked.

You may have time,
but probably not.

You may have months, or even years, before you need to get your first client.

If you are in that position, great! No rush to learn the skills to fill your diary with engagements.

We have options in our careers.

Option #1: Keep dreaming about the business we've always wanted, a want-a-preneur. Create big goals and expectations, and then do nothing. Live with our message and potential trapped inside of us.

Option #2: Take action on our speaking career. Start booking speaking engagements now. Stand on stages and make an impact with our message.

Option #2 sounds better, doesn't it? That is why you are reading this book.

So how do we get our first speaking client? Our first booking?

It isn't as hard or scary as we think.

We don't have to become internet marketers, copywriting experts, or take three years to get a degree in graphic design.

We don't need to sell our souls, work for free, or live off the scraps by being a side act in someone else's show.

We can take simple steps towards our goal of a full-time speaking career, and focus on what we do best: Speaking to audiences.

Let's get some bookings.

Well, this should be easy. Just pick up the phone, call an organization that could use my wonderful services, and say, "Please connect me to the person in charge of hiring great speakers."

Bernie, Mark, and Tom are still waiting for that to work.

Or, how about this?

Cold prospecting.

We search Google and find the email addresses of event planners. Then we send them an email that says, "I see that you've hired speakers in the past. I am a good speaker, please hire me."

Yes, this will fail too.

This has probably worked for someone at some time, but the odds are against us. Plus, we don't want to spend the rest of our life sending unanswered emails, or being a telemarketer.

Now, if we are currently a skilled telemarketer and enjoy the grind of phone call after phone call, great. Continue down this path. But for most of us mere mortals, we want to be speakers and not telemarketers.

We can do better than cold telemarketing.

Let's explore many of the better ways we can get bookings now.

One of these ways may be perfect for you!

#1. The "laser approach."

Why compete with the competition, when we can make ourselves the only choice?

In 2012 Kevin Kruse wrote the book, *Employee Engagement 2.0: How to Motivate Your Team for High Performance (A "Real-World" Guide for Busy Managers)*. The book didn't sell a lot of copies.

But that isn't why Kevin wrote the book.

Kevin knew this was a hot topic in corporate America. Large corporations needed keynote speeches and training in this area. Where would they look for speakers on this topic? The Internet, of course. And guess which book showed up at the top of the Google search for the term "employee engagement?"

You guessed it. Kevin's book.

Why such a high ranking on Google? First, the title of the book perfectly matched many corporate searches for the topic. Second, the book was available on Amazon, which carries a lot of weight in search engines.

So who got the highly-paid speaking engagements on this trendy corporate topic? Kevin.

When we laser-focus our marketing to our target audience (in this case, event planners doing internet searches for speakers on a specific topic), we make it easy for event planners to choose us.

Now, who could we laser-target our speaking or training to? Here are some ideas.

"I don't have any leads!"

At our local networking event, we visit with a local salesman. The salesman complains, "I don't have any leads! My presentation is great, but I have no one to talk to. My company's advertising is not working."

This salesman's company has a problem. If we have the skills to hold a workshop or coaching session on getting leads, we can fix this problem. No one else is proposing a solution to the problem. We would be the only ones.

Our contact message would be simple:

"Does your company have a problem getting more leads for your salespeople? I can fix that problem."

The company can make an instant decision. If they want to fix their problem, we are the only solution.

Done.

Manager and employee retreats.

There are many hotels and conference centers that host manager and employee retreats. Companies invest tens of thousands of dollars to get their teams to work together. What do we know about these companies?

They already invest time and money to solve their problems. Is our option less expensive? Does it require fewer days away from work? Can we provide better results?

It isn't hard to get the names of these companies. Hotels and conference centers list their events in their lobby, and usually on their websites too. Don't know who to approach? Simple. Ask one of the attendees during the break.

Now, think about this. Companies will run a boring event. Lots of company data and training. But, they could do that at the office. Why did they travel and have a special event away from their work location?

Inspiration and motivation. They want to inspire and motivate the team to work together and to get improved results.

If the company bosses speak at the event, the managers and employees will think, "I have heard it all before." They need someone from the outside to get their attention. That would be us.

We could even tell the group the same message they have heard so many times before, but we are a different voice. They will pay attention to us.

If the bosses could inspire and motivate the team at the office, they would not need this event away from work. They need us.

Trade shows and exhibitions.

We create these opportunities with our imagination. We find an event that already has an audience, but doesn't have speakers. Here is an example.

Trade show organizers have two basic income sources. First, they sell tickets to attendees of the event. Second, they sell booth space to exhibitors.

The easiest part of the event for organizers is selling booth space. Businesses desperately want to get in front of more prospects. The hardest part for the event organizers is to get attendees.

The more attendees there are, the easier it will be for organizers to sell their high-priced booths to exhibitors.

As a speaker, we can give attendees one more reason to attend. We can offer them education.

Tom approached a small business opportunity trade show. Their Saturday/Sunday event toured the United States and Canada, 26 weekends a year. Tom proposed to the organizer that he could do two 45-minute workshops a day, one in the morning, and one in the afternoon.

- The workshops would attract more attendees, and increase the organizer's revenue.

- More attendees meant it would make exhibition booths easier to sell.

- Attendees might stay at the event all day to attend both workshops. This would make the event appear more crowded and exciting.

He closed the booking by asking for an exhibition booth as total payment for his speaking fee. The extra exhibition booth cost the organizer nothing. He was thrilled. While Tom did not attend all 26 yearly events, he attended those that made sense for his schedule.

What could be the benefits from this arrangement? We could:

- Sell at our exhibition booth.

- Sell our exhibition booth space to someone else.

- Get consulting clients from the attendees at our talks.

- Get new coaching clients.

- Get future bookings for our speeches from attendees that were impressed with our knowledge.
- Visit with the people at the other exhibition booths to network for future speaking opportunities.
- We could even ask for the mailing list of the attendees from the organizer if that would benefit us.

This list could go on and on, but we get the idea.

How many events do not have education opportunities for attendees?

How many events could use an entertaining speaker?

How many events could benefit from our break-out instructional workshops?

How many trade shows and exhibitions are there in our area? Let's list a few.

- Job fairs.
- Career fairs.
- Home shows.
- Auto shows.
- Electronics shows.
- Agricultural shows.
- Sports memorabilia shows.
- Antique shows.
- Food shows.
- Fashion shows.
- Printing equipment exhibitions.

- Medical equipment exhibitions.

- Flea markets. (Yes, think creatively.)

- Health food shows.

- Furniture shows.

- And so many more.

If we can't find a trade show or exhibition, we are not trying. At the time of this writing, a quick search on Google shows one site with 10,376 scheduled trade shows and exhibitions listed. Since some shows have multiple events, this site lists over 20,648 scheduled events. Certainly that's enough for us to choose from.

There are even trade shows, conferences, and events about being a trade show organizer!

If we can't find a trade show or exhibition that works for us, we can create our own.

Here is an example.

Let's say we speak about self-image for teenagers. Maybe we have scheduled times for our courses, or possibly do individual coaching. We create a teen modeling fashion show event. Plenty of teens volunteer to be models. The local shopping mall hosts and advertises the event. Volunteers from the local community college business class organize everything, and we speak at the event.

We created the audience for our speech that leads to coaching, or students for our self-image classes.

Tom personally organized several small tradeshows and had up to eight different speakers at the show. The attendees stayed all day at the show and loved it. The exhibitors loved that the attendees stayed the entire day, so that they could speak to them in depth. It was a win-win for everyone.

Need more examples of where to look for shows?

- Suppose we speak about pet psychology. How many pet shows are there in our local area? How many giant pet stores could use our speech to attract people to their stores on Saturday? How many veterinarian conferences could we attend?

- Suppose we speak to or coach managers. At a health and wellness exhibition, we could have a workshop titled, "How to handle stress for managers." Only a small percentage of the attendees qualify to attend. But, wouldn't these be the exact people we would want to talk to? And we have them all in one place.

- Suppose we speak to or coach high-performers. Think high-end watch and jewelry shows. A percentage of the audience could be our perfect prospects.

It is so easy to get booked at conferences. Many don't have speaking budgets, but they do have the right audience for us. This could be the cheapest advertising and promotion we could ever do. Many of the right people are in our audience to see us at our best. And as a huge bonus, we have no competition.

There are big shows, small shows, regional shows, and shows that we can't imagine. Once we know our targeted audience, choosing shows to contact gets easier.

A quick tip. Try to speak early in the day. This will give us more credibility and fame when we talk to attendees at our booth, and also to the other exhibitors.

Direct email.

Early in the blockchain and cryptocurrency excitement, Mark saw an online promotion for an upcoming event in Manila, Philippines.

These events always had the same problem. No professional host or emcee. They feature credible computer scientists as expert speakers. At the last moment, many of these scientists get cold feet and don't even come to the event. Nerdy computer scientists seldom speak in front of groups. They finish early, or they run too late with 137 slides in their presentation. Nothing runs on time.

Sometimes the emcee would introduce the next speaker, then there would be silence. The speaker disappeared. Mark knew he could fill these gaps and keep the conference moving forward.

With a cold email, he messaged the organizer. Well, not entirely cold. Mark did a little research and made sure he had the organizer's name spelled correctly. Instead of a demo video, Mark sent links to past industry events that he had appeared in. Instant credibility.

Organizers don't plan. They don't want to deal with the scheduling and no-show speaker problems. Mark's offer made it easy.

He offered to emcee their two-day event for 500 people in Manila, Philippines, for free. The organizer would simply provide his airline ticket. In return, the organizer would give Mark a fully-paid speaking spot two weeks later in Ho Chi Minh City, Vietnam. Mark loves to travel.

At the end of day one, there was a networking meeting for the attendees to meet and chat. Instead of hiding in his hotel room like most speakers or emcees after an event, Mark participated to meet some of the attendees. And guess what? Mark met another gentleman who ran small conferences in Hong Kong and South Korea. Two months later, Mark was conducting a seminar in Seoul from this new contact.

What made this easy? Mark has a good hook. Most conferences in the financial services industry are boring. He makes them interesting. He covers for speakers who don't show up. He takes care of the details for the organizer. And he hosts panels. That is an irresistible offer.

When we meet people at networking events, our first few sentences need to be effective. We will want to perfect and practice our hook well in advance of meeting these people.

What was the grand total of paid speaking events for Mark that came from offering to emcee for free?

- Three days of paid speaking in the Philippines.
- Two days of paid speaking in Vietnam.
- Two days of paid speaking in South Korea.
- Three days of paid speaking in Indonesia.

The lesson? After speaking, we shouldn't hide in our hotel room and rest. It is better to network and visit with the audience. What a good place to find opportunities to speak! And if we did a spectacular job in our speech, it gets easier to get instant bookings.

Event organizers are desperate to book interesting speakers who provide valuable content.

There are always more promoters than good speakers. It won't take long to build a reputation so that we can be in demand.

Booking the big stage.

In the financial services industry, there is a big annual conference called the MDRT (Million Dollar Round Table). Bernie's goal? To be a main speaker at the Hong Kong event.

Step #1: If we don't know the organizer, we have to find someone who does. That is the easiest entry into a conversation.

Bernie spoke at a UK Personal Finance Society event. While talking to the organizer, the organizer mentioned, "I will be having a meeting with someone from the MDRT." Bernie asked the organizer for an introduction.

Step #2: It took several follow-up phone calls, but eventually, Bernie was able to contact the person in charge of speakers. The rest was easy. Bernie's background, his website, his best-selling book, and famous testimonials secured the speaking slot. We don't have all of these things when we start, but the lesson is to start accumulating these credibility pieces now. They will make future bookings easy.

Ah, but it gets better.

Step #3: Bernie contacted financial services companies in Hong Kong and China. Email and cold calls work if we have a compelling offer. Bernie's offer?

"I can train and speak to your sales organization in Hong Kong and China on the following dates. I will already be in the area for my speaking appearance at the MDRT. You do not need to pay for my flight. You do not have to pay for my hotel. I am saving you £4000. All you have to do is pay for my time."

When we remove barriers, it is easier for organizers to make quick decisions.

Bernie uses this strategy again and again. When a company has a low budget, he reaches out to similar companies in the area who can at least afford his speaking fee. The companies are happy to save money on their training budget, and Bernie is happy about filling his speaking diary.

A word of warning.

Most speakers and coaches do this. They think,

"I have this speech or this training course. Where can I find people who want it?"

That is a very difficult approach. Instead, let's consider this approach.

"What is a problem that people want to solve?"

There is a never-ending list out there. With a clear problem in mind, we can take what we know and speak about and make it into an attractive solution.

Even then, there is good news and bad news.

The bad news? We will waste time marketing our solution to people who don't want to solve their problems.

Many people and organizations have problems that they do not want to solve. Attempting to sell them on our services leads to quick rejection and failure.

Some examples of this?

Maybe a company thinks this: "Our employees tell us they need leadership training. But if they begin to think like leaders, they may leave us for other more attractive companies. Let's put off that training until next year instead."

Or maybe we offer sales training?

Our potential client thinks, "Yes, we have a sales problem. But the market is down, and now is not a good time to use our company's money on training. We won't get any more sales in today's market. Let us preserve what we have and wait for our competitors to suffer."

The good news is that most companies and organizations **do** want to solve their problems. Let's work with them.

But what if I am only a coach?

Imagine a worst-case scenario. If we can fix this terrible scenario, everything will feel easy.

What is the hardest question we might have?

"Getting clients is hopeless. How do I start? I teach a boring, generic leadership course to managers. They can't measure the benefit of my course or coaching for months. I am not allowed to change the content. My target market doesn't know me or respect me. So how do I sell that?"

Yes, that is a bad scenario. Let's fix it now.

We have many problems here.

- We are a "nobody."

- They don't know we even exist.

- They don't know that they need us.

- They don't feel that they have a problem.

- We can't guarantee measurable results.

This is like pushing a giant boulder uphill. But, if we are committed to this challenge, let's get to work. The solution is not fast or easy. This could be our step-by-step strategy.

1. We have to go from "nobody" to "somebody." Writing a book would give us instant credibility. Can't do that? Write a special report that helps solve a particular industry problem. Can't do that? Get some testimonials from previous clients raving about the results. Don't have

previous clients? Maybe we'll have to offer a free course to a client in exchange for testimonials.

2. Get exposure to our potential clients. We can send them our special report. Give them a copy of our book. If we send a testimonial, make sure our testimonial mentions some value or skill they can use immediately. It is easier to approach potential clients when we've already established a relationship.

3. Educate our potential clients about the problems we've solved. Let them know they are living with these problems right now. Show the harm to productivity or revenue that will come from keeping these problems.

These first three strategies? We call this "creating clients" instead of "finding clients." If we have even a small relationship with our potential clients, it is easier to approach them and communicate with them.

But what about that guarantee that first-time clients might want?

If we can't guarantee measurable results, what should we do? An increase in sales is easy to measure. Reducing customer service complaints is easy to measure.

Leadership and better cooperation among employees are harder to measure. This is where glowing testimonials help.

But what if the client insists on a guarantee? They might think, "Why should I take a chance and risk my money on you?"

If we are not confident that what we provide will have measurable results, we could at least guarantee this:

"If you don't see the results, I will come back, retrain, and coach the group again, completely at my expense."

Does this sound like a lot of work? Yes. But, we can do it.

If we are not willing to invest that much time to get a client, we have choices.

- We could choose a different target market.

- We could change what we teach or coach.

- We could step back and repackage what we offer to provide a clearer value to potential clients.

- We could change our description of what we offer.

- And of course, we can make the decision or buying process simpler for potential clients.

Every day clients spend money to solve their problems. If we properly position ourselves and what we offer, we will get our share of the market. But we don't want to make this hard on ourselves. There are easier ways to do this.

#2. Instant bookings.

Mark wanted to tour the United Kingdom. He marketed a series of open-to-the-public events from Scotland to the south of England. He booked his workshops every other day. Why?

At the end of each workshop, Mark announced that he had the following day available for anyone that would like him to speak to their company or group. First-come, first-served. The attendees loved his workshop, and booking the following day was easy. Since only one or two people could book their group for the next day, the scarcity of Mark's time created instant decisions and commitments.

Same transportation expense for Mark, but twice as many workshops.

His workshop schedule listed each event for the week. Any attendee could share the schedule. Each subsequent event had more attendees. One person attended four out of the five events during that tour. This one enthusiastic attendee brought more people to the different events. Mark's approach generated over £2,000 extra registration income, just from one attendee's recommendations.

So how did Mark get his first speaking opportunity?

Before Mark started his public speaking career, he sold self-improvement books at large conferences.

One nutrition company conducted events for their sales-people in different cities every month. While selling books in the back of the room at one of their New Zealand events, the emcee asked Mark to come to the front and say something about the books for sale. Mark only spoke for five minutes. Since Mark did a good job for those five minutes, this arrangement continued for future events.

In time, this positioned Mark as an expert in the self-improvement industry. As his reputation grew, the company asked Mark to speak at some of their smaller events. It was a start. The speaking fee was minimal, but sales of books increased. Most of his money came from the sales of his book inventory.

Mark knew the value of the audience, and accepted the token speaking fee. He increased his range of products for sale, and made more and more money every time he jumped on a plane.

More risk reversal?

Here is another example of an instant booking. The key? Removing the risk for the organizer.

It's Saturday. Bernie is on a train full of Manchester United supporters, excited about the big game. As a fan, Bernie has something in common with everyone on the train. Starting conversations is easy.

While chatting with the stranger across the aisle, Bernie learns that he sells small franchises for his core business. The man is quite successful. He has 200 franchisees of his business already.

Bernie: "Fantastic. You have 200 franchisees already."

Stranger: "When things are good, yes. But when things are bad, it is horrible. They quit. And then they demand their £5000 back that they originally invested with us."

Bernie: "I am just curious. Do they want to quit their franchise because they can't get enough customers?"

Stranger: "Yes. I hate giving them their money back. That means we both lost time and effort."

Bernie: "Do you have any trainings or events for them?"

Stranger: "Yes. We do quarterly events with all 200 franchisees attending."

Bernie: "Well, if I could speak to them, and teach them how to get more customers, would that help you?"

Stranger: (Instant objection) "I don't have any budget for a speaker."

Bernie: "How about this? I will take the whole risk. What if I create an audio training CD and a booklet to help them get more customers? Value of £20. And, I'll sell these to you for only £10. Would that help you and make you look good in their eyes?"

Stranger: "Yes!"

Done.

Then they both laughed at how easily they found a solution. The train arrived at the stadium. While getting off the train, Bernie shook hands, introduced himself, and gave the stranger his business card.

They could chat about the location and the time later. Now, it was time to focus on the big game.

Let's do the math.

200 people. Bernie receives £2,000 for some CDs and booklets. After production expenses, Bernie nets £1,000 for his speaking

fee. For the organizer, no net cost. He added £20 to the cost of each attendee's ticket for the event. No risks for the organizer, and a "free" speaker/trainer for his event.

Now, here is where it gets interesting. Bernie amazed the attendees with his word-for-word solutions on getting new customers. The best advertising we can ever have is always a great speech or training.

Bernie had additional audios in the back of the room that many purchased. They were eager to learn more. This added another £4000 in profit for Bernie.

Plus, many attendees insisted on personally becoming a one-on-one coaching client.

Math is so much fun.

Instant booking from current business.

This way is very simple. Tom taught a sales training class. What would be a good way to see if his training worked?

Challenge the sales class to put their new skills to use.

He asked them, "Did you improve your sales skills in this class?" Of course they did. They loved the magic words and phrases. So, Tom continued, "Would you like to learn more skills?" Again, they agreed.

Then he challenged them. "Here is a test of your new skills. Sell your boss that you want to learn more."

Easy. The next class sold out and was scheduled for the next day.

Talk to the organizer.

Bernie spoke at a large insurance event. But, he was only one of many speakers. The stars that attracted the attendees were the Olympic athletes and the celebrities.

Now, here is where it gets interesting. Bernie was a "minor" speaker at the event. He delivered hard core, word-for-word skills. The audience loved it and took notes furiously. His material was exactly what they needed to get better results.

The "major speakers" did their prepared, canned speeches about general motivation. Many people in the audience spent that time checking their messages.

Guess who the attendees lined up for pictures with? Bernie.

On the day after the event at the sponsors' luncheon, Bernie approached the event organizer. Why at the end? The event was over. Now the organizer could finally relax. While many of the other speakers flew home, Bernie stayed behind to see if he could add any extra value for the organizers.

They asked Bernie if he could stay over and speak at another event the next day. Bernie accepted. They loved Bernie's talk the day before. And they hired Bernie for several years in a row.

Timing is important. We don't want to talk to an event organizer until they can focus on what we can do for them. Wait until the end of a busy event, or immediately after, if we want the event organizer's full attention.

So what did Bernie say at the luncheon? If someone had a problem, he replied, "Perhaps I could demonstrate one of my quick training tips that could help fix this."

A few sentences later, they asked if Bernie would also speak the next day.

The keynote speaker becomes the in-house trainer.

A small nutrition company booked Mark as the keynote speaker for their annual conference. Tiny budget, small speaking fee. Only 40 women showed up. On the plus side, Mark could sell books to the conference attendees in the back of the room during the breaks.

After Mark's keynote speech, the company's sales manager made Mark an offer. She said, "We need someone to regularly visit the major cities and provide training for our sales reps. We will pay your travel expenses, but we can't afford another corporate salary. Instead, we can offer a commission on the increase in sales you help our salespeople achieve."

Commission only?

Let's see how this stacks up.

1. The company pays Mark's travel expenses around Australia and New Zealand. Mark travels for free.

2. The company is okay with Mark doing his own private events while he is in each city.

3. The company gets their salespeople to attend Mark's company training. Mark can sell books to the attendees.

4. If sales increase, Mark gets a commission.

The sales manager was keen to get someone on the road to motivate and inspire the sales force, as her family commitments meant she couldn't travel. This was a win-win for everyone.

Overnight, the company experienced a sales boom. Mark received nice commission checks. However, this would be a win-win proposition, even without a commission.

The no-risk approach.

Everyone loves a win-win situation.

Independent financial advisors are everywhere in England. They want more skills and better results.

The caller asked Bernie, "So how much is your speaking fee?"

Bernie sensed the caller was on a budget. On the plus side, the event was local. No travel. He could fit it in during an afternoon. 120 individual advisors would be in attendance.

Bernie replied, "I will make this very easy for you. If I speak at no cost, would I be able to promote an audio training album that can help the advisors make more sales if they like what they learned? That way you get me to speak for free. And if I am any good, the audio album will give them more techniques to get more clients. Then you win both ways."

Bernie took all the risk.

Out of 120 people in the audience, 60 people wanted an album. That led to £3000 in immediate sales from the event. Plus, Bernie let the audience know he did coaching too.

Ten years later, Bernie is still working with the group.

We want to speak, but who cares?

Our passion is speaking. We enthusiastically deliver our mes-sage. We find fulfillment in front of an adoring audience.

But no one cares about us and what we want. No one wants to hear our tragic story or our personal therapy.

Clients don't care about our passion for speaking. They care about their results and outcomes.

But what if we are an awesome speaker?

The best speakers in the world get Toastmaster ribbons. The best marketers get paid speaking events.

These are two different skills.

Skill #1. Good speaking and presentation skills.

Skill #2. Marketing ourselves to get paid speaking events.

This book is about Skill #2. If we want to fill our diary with paid speaking events, we must stop thinking about ourselves. Instead, we must think about what our potential clients want. We want to be fully-employed, not under-employed.

Speakers ... speak.

If we don't speak, we are only part of an audience.

It will take marketing to accumulate paid speaking engage-ments. If marketing scares us, let's reframe how we think about marketing.

Instead of pushy, sleazy selling, let's imagine marketing as communicating our value to others. Then, when potential organizers see our marketing, we will be the answer to what they want and need.

What will we market?

1. Our talent, knowledge, and expertise.

2. Our clear and effective delivery.

3. Our message.

4. Our image.

We'll talk more about how we will market ourselves in a moment. But for now, think about these exposures to potential organizers:

1. Our YouTube video of the best moments in our speeches.

2. Our website.

3. Our offer of value to potential organizers.

4. Testimonials.

5. Proof of results.

6. An easy sound bite or hook that describes what we deliver.

7. Our book or published industry articles.

These exposures will be easier to create when we understand **what** our potential organizers **want**. Here is how we should look at event organizers:

1. Event organizers don't want to pay us to speak.

2. However, they love to pay us for results.

If we focus on the event organizer's problems, and then successfully deliver results, we will never be unemployed.

Then what should we talk about?

We should speak about what our target market wants. Hopefully, we already have our audience-centered topic or speech. If not? Then now would be the time to rethink what we speak about.

We want our passion or skills to correlate with what our market wants. As we know, there are plenty of markets for almost any passion or skill.

The only caution is that we don't want to end up with a topic no one wants to hear about. No amount of advertising and promotion will fix this problem.

"But what if I spend my entire life creating this 45-minute speech that no one seems to want?"

Don't despair. Sometimes changing the title of our speech is all we need to do. Imagine our speech title was, "Best practices for managers and supervisors." Not a bad title, but no one wants to hire us.

But let's say we change the title of our speech to, "How to get employees to listen to their managers and supervisors." Not a big change. But maybe event organizers will think, "That sounds interesting for the attendees. They would love this."

Same speech, different title.

Now, let's take a deeper look into our topic and potential market.

What do we have to offer?

Imagine we are a certified trainer for an educational or vocational skills course. Then, we know exactly what we will talk about. We just need a business audience.

Do we have an uplifting, inspirational message that motivates people to leave our talk ready to take action? This opens up a bigger market for us. Charities want their donors to take action and donate immediately. Businesses want their employees to change their behaviors and work together more efficiently. Sales managers want their salespeople to immediately get more appointments.

Do we have a unique skill or knowledge that can immediately change people's lives?

Do we have a common negative experience that we overcame, and that others might like to hear about? For example, how to take care of our elderly parents when they can no longer take care of themselves. Or, how to fix our negative credit. Or even how to get a date when the Internet has failed us.

If our passion is speaking to high schoolers about vocational options, we would look for new, illustrative stories and options to present. We know our message.

We will want to make our message as commercial as possible.

Why?

Because it is easier to get booked and **paid** for business speaking events than for an inspirational speech. Businesses have money. They will invest money, if we can deliver more value than our speaking fee.

Should we ignore charities, schools, and inspirational speaking events? Of course not. However, if we want to fill our speaking diary with speaking appearances, businesses have an unlimited appetite for speakers who deliver great value.

What shouldn't we speak about?

If we want to relive our trauma in front of an audience, we better hope our story of trauma has a message or lesson. No one wants to hear speakers complain about how hard their lives have been.

Remember, speaking isn't about us. It is about our audience. When we focus on our audience, our market becomes easier to see.

Hmmm. Then what should we speak about?

Let's take a look at a few markets. These are not the only markets, but it gives us an idea of how huge the potential is for our speaking services.

Topics for business.

Let's start with business topics. Businesses are in the business of making a profit. They are willing to invest money in a speaker if the speaker can give them a good return on their investment.

Yes, if we help businesses make more money, we will fill our diary. Businesses know how to earn money. If they can trade $5,000 for our time, but get $10,000 in more business profits, the choice is clear. Businesses will do this as often as they can.

Imagine a business decision-maker sitting at his desk thinking, "Let me organize a huge group so the speaker will have an audience. I know this will make the speaker feel good and fulfilled."

Doesn't happen.

What do decision-makers want?

They want their problems solved.

What kind of problems do decision-makers have?

Here are a few of the thousands of areas that we could specialize in for business.

Employee motivation.

Employees show up late, call in sick, don't take responsibility, do substandard work, don't communicate, and fight with their fellow employees.

Not all employees are like this, of course. However, enough employees do this to give businesses headaches. Can we do something about this? Do we have a message or training that will improve the situation?

Managers teach their employees, but most employees don't listen. Yet, the same employees listen and take action on the same message when it is presented by a stranger. Can we be that stranger?

Companies always need an "outsider" to inspire their employees to change. The companies' executives can't be the surprise inspirational speaker themselves.

Managers.

Some managers are good at spreadsheets, but terrible with people. Their person-to-person skills are awful. Not only do they de-motivate employees, but they have no idea why. They think employees should feel fulfilled because they get a paycheck.

Or maybe these managers feel frustrated. They are told to achieve unreasonable results with inadequate resources. Or even worse, they are given responsibility without the authority to make it happen.

Where do most managers come from? From good employees who have good employee skills. As a reward, many businesses promote them to a manager's job, where they have no skills, training, or experience. What could go wrong? A lot.

Know how to make a manager speechless? Ask a manager, "What do you say to inspire an unmotivated employee?"

Managers need to excel in inspiration, teamwork, managing problems, and more. They don't get these skills by accepting a promotion. They won't get these skills from the company policy manual. Do we see a market yet?

Salespeople and sales managers.

For salespeople, what is the reward for working hard and having an outstanding year? Bigger quotas and sales goals for the following year. If salespeople work at 100% capacity with their current skills, the only way for them to improve is with new skills.

What about sales managers? The company's future rests on them. No sales? No future. Sales managers need help. Limited budgets, unrealistic quotas, untrained or unmotivated sales staff, and fierce competition are a few of the challenges in today's market. Their sales staff may be deaf to their pleas of higher sales, more appointments, or better closing ratios. This is where we come in. We could be the outside voice that the staff will hear.

Salespeople need new skills for a rapidly-changing marketplace. The sales managers and upper-level managers won't have these skills. They have jobs. They don't have time to keep up with the newest and latest changes.

Investor conferences.

They have the budget. Many conduct their conferences in exotic destinations.

Most conferences at these exotic locations are not about secret, deep-dive, complicated investment strategies. Instead, they get "big picture" talks by celebrities, overviews on new regulations, a few awards, etc.

Can our message enhance their conferences? Are we an expert in these types of investments? Or, are we the entertainment? Maybe we are the emcee that makes the event move at an interesting pace instead of dragging to a boring end.

Creative and IT staff.

Social media, new trends, increased competition, and changing media outlets challenge the creative and marketing departments. For IT, their world is constantly changing. How do they keep up? Conferences and conventions where they exchange experiences and ideas with their peers.

These conference and convention organizers know that amateur speakers can discourage their audiences and endanger the future of their events. They need professional speakers for emcees, content, and of course, entertainment.

Can you imagine a conference where every speaker was an introverted programmer? Of course not.

Don't forget training.

Mark filled four days of his week for years with employee training for franchises. Small franchise owners don't have the time, expertise, or budget to hire a full-time trainer. To get their employees trained and certified, they depend on outside trainers.

These trainings happened during the weekdays. This left Mark's weekends free to do keynote speeches at larger conferences.

Bernie fills his week with training workshops and coaching. After a three-hour training workshop, many attendees request personal one-on-one coaching sessions.

The secret? Make sure the training sessions are awesome. The new skills have to put money in the attendees' pockets.

When a company sees instant results, the company immediately books multiple trainings for all of their locations.

But back to the secret.

If the content is fresh, innovative, tested, proven, and gets awesome results, we can let our content do our advertising. Future bookings are easy.

The best advertising and promotion we will ever do is give an awesome talk that delivers true value.

Trade associations.

How many trades have local, regional and national events? Every trade from plumbers, restaurant managers, roofing contractors, to firefighters and beyond.

- Are we an expert on new industry regulations?
- Could we be the futurist who gives them direction about where their industry is headed?
- Do we specialize in giving advice?
- Are we the inspirational entertainment for their after-dinner speech?
- Or at worst, can we hand out awards and trophies?

Don't assume the current employees at the Trade Association headquarters are qualified to fill these roles. Most will want to hire professionals for these roles.

One of our friends, Mike, made a living speaking to conferences for owners of small storage unit sites. Owners might have 50 to 200 units for rent. People will rent a storage unit to store everything they can't fit into their garages or apartments. A niche market? Certainly.

Mike's speaking fees were modest. His income came from his specialized software for the owners, and future training. Because he was the speaker, the owners instantly trusted Mike and his recommendations.

Entrepreneurs.

This is a huge audience.

What do we know about entrepreneurs?

They have a huge desire to create and build a business. Unfortunately, they may not have the necessary skills to make this happen. Entrepreneurs love to attend conferences and training events. Can we think of a few niche markets for speaking to entrepreneurs?

- Amazon marketplace sellers.
- Freelance web designers.
- Advertising and marketing consultants.
- Network marketers.
- Independent sales reps.
- IT consultants.
- Bookkeepers and tax preparers.
- Home repair contractors.
- Independent insurance agents.
- Lawncare and landscaping owners.

Oh, we've only scratched the surface!

Let's look at some other popular booking opportunities.

Businesses are not the only places where we can earn paying speaking opportunities.

Under-financed charities.

Giving away money is easy. But to raise funds for charities, it takes a special message.

Do the charity directors feel they have the charisma and professional presenting skills to get audiences to donate?

Charities have a mission, but they need us to present that mission in a clear way to others.

Annual Christmas dinners or business retreats?

Speakers provide variety at corporate functions. We might be the featured benefit that draws employees to the function.

Building a speech that displays a fresh voice to everyone at the workplace is a great way to get more of these speaking engagements.

The education market?

Not the highest-paying speaking fees, but maybe this is our passion. Of course, if we are a former president or prime minister, we could command huge fees. From 2001 to 2016, Bill and Hillary Clinton received over $150 million in speaking fees, mostly from corporations. But, there were many universities in their schedule. The universities paid speaking fees to the Clinton Foundation that averaged between $100,000 to $250,000 per speech.

Schools are easy to find. We don't have to guess what their business is. Many schools have listings online of various administrators and departments.

But who hires speakers at the schools? Research would be easy. Talk to a few people at the school and find out who hired the last speaker for the assembly. Get an appointment to talk to that person to find out the criteria for hiring an outside speaker.

This process is easy because we focused only on the school market. We didn't stand in the middle of the street wondering where we could speak.

Schools constantly hire speakers. We could spend our entire career in education if that was our passion.

Political causes. Environmental causes. Community movements.

We only have to look at social media to see huge movements to get others to change their views.

Think of the best climate change scientists in the world. Are they trained communicators who can deliver their message effectively? Rarely. Their expertise is science. We can be their spokesperson.

If we are new, start small. Talk to the local chapter. Find out when their upcoming events occur. Do they have speakers booked yet? What are they looking for? What problems do they have? How can we help?

If we help one local chapter, other chapters will want us. Then, it won't be hard to move up the ladder to state conventions and more.

Remember, we might be the difference between an uninspiring fundraising event, and a brilliant fundraising event that sets records. Delivering a professional message that touches the hearts of the audience makes a difference.

Health organizations?

A huge portion of national expenditures goes to health.

Think hospitals, health initiatives, health education, cancer associations, diabetes associations, and more.

How many conferences are there for doctors, hospital administrators, nurses, pharmaceutical salespeople, equipment manufacturers, etc?

Weight loss? That market always demands new, inspirational speakers and instructors. Do we have experience or knowledge in this area? This market will not go away or go out of style. Overweight people will always want to hear a new approach.

Do we teach an innovative way for diabetics to control their blood sugar levels? This market is growing.

Health fairs and exhibitions attract lots of attendees. We can enhance the events.

Master of ceremonies.

Recognition award events can be boring. The master of ceremonies creates interesting dialogue between the awards. Now the experience comes alive for the attendees. A great master of ceremonies will make the organizer look brilliant.

Will this pay handsomely?

Probably not.

However, important decision-makers will see us at the event. We get paid, while creating free advertising for our services.

The market awaits us.

Yes, we recognize that unlimited speaking opportunities exist, but none of this matters unless …

We get booked!

It's easy to see that we only began with a few speaking markets. The list can go on and on. But there is a huge difference between market potential, and getting a paid booking to speak.

Now, back to more ways to get bookings.

#3. Use the speaker network.

In 2006, Mark had never visited Budapest, Hungary. In fact, he didn't know a single Hungarian citizen. But in the following years, he became a speaking sensation, and not only in Hungary, but Romania, Slovakia, and other neighboring countries. Companies used Mark's services as an emcee at conventions, for keynotes, and for training days. How did he do this?

With the speaker network.

What is the speaker network?

Imagine we speak for a company convention. The company may love us, but they don't want us for next year's event. They don't want to announce to the delegates, "Hey, we have the same keynote speaker again." The delegates want someone new.

So the company says to us, "Hey. Great job. Loved your talk. So who could you recommend for our event next year?"

Well, what would we say? "Well, if you are not inviting me, I won't help you. I will make you search through speakers and you can just hope they don't do a bad job." No, I don't think we would say that.

Instead, we recommend someone we personally know who will do a great job for their next convention. And in return, I am sure the event planner would give us a glowing testimonial letter about our performance at this year's event.

And that is what happened to Mark. The previous speaker at the company event recommended Mark for the promoter's next event in Hungary.

If we create a network of other speakers that we respect and trust, we will pre-sell their services to our current event planner. And yes, they will do the same for us.

Event planners want variety. If we are a trainer, we can't be present at every training event. There are many opportunities for us to recommend other speakers, trainers, and coaches. It takes only a few seconds. We should recommend others everywhere we go.

We will create our own network of speakers who have the trust of their existing clients. Their clients then reach out to us based upon their recommendation.

This eliminates prospecting as we build our speaker network over time.

Here are a few reasons that we, or our speaker network friends, turn down speaking opportunities and recommend their speaker friends.

- Our happy client does not want us back. They want someone new.
- We don't want to travel on that day or to that location.
- Our speaker friend lives closer.
- We don't feel comfortable with the training they want.
- The speaking fee is too low for us, but okay for a speaking friend.
- We already have a booking for the date they want.

- We didn't connect or enjoy our relationship with the event organizer.

How do we develop a speaker network?

Easy. Start recommending. Every new connection we make continues our personal network.

And when we do a great job, make sure we take a few seconds to recommend one of our speaker friends for their next event.

The minimum requirement for entry as a professional speaker.

Not a celebrity?

Not a world-famous athlete?

Not a New York Times best-selling author?

Not a former president?

Not a famous scientist with the cure for cancer?

In this case, we have to sell ourselves.

Imagine this scenario. The convention ends. The final keynote speaker bombs. Everyone leaves depressed.

The CEO takes the event planner aside and says, "The final speaker was horrible. Why did you hire this person? You were in charge and turned this convention into a disaster."

The event planner gulps and replies, "I didn't check the speaker out. I'd never heard the speaker before, but the brochure looked good."

This never happens. Event planners want to keep their jobs. So before we get hired to speak, they will want proof that we can deliver.

We are not going to get hired because our friend said to the event planner, "I have a friend that speaks really well." No, that isn't enough to get booked.

Marketing begins with us asking the question, "How will people find me?"

So what is the minimum that event planners will look for?

Let us look at some ways we can help ourselves.

A website.

If we are just starting, we might get away with a Facebook business page, or even a LinkedIn profile. But, websites are easy today. Freelancers can produce an acceptable website inexpensively, so why not invest in one right now?

The purpose of our website is not to educate or entertain our potential audience. Instead, we will create our website to sell event planners on our services.

What will we need? Here are four basic elements:

1. Our picture.

2. Our topic or skill.

3. Our demo video.

4. Our contact information.

This could all be on one page.

Shouldn't we have a page where they can download our different profile pictures? A lead capture form? A page for testimonials? A page to list the prestigious speaking events we've participated in? A list of our awards and accomplishments?

These things are nice. But they are not necessary to start. We can grow into that.

Don't let a year of our lives slip away while we design the perfect webpage. Take action now and at least do the minimum for entry into the world of public speaking.

Let's look at these four basic elements on our website.

#1. Our picture.

Our high school graduation photo? Of course not. Our vacation picture hanging off the edge of the Grand Canyon? Only if we are speaking about daredevil techniques or adventure travel.

A professional headshot by a professional photographer will make us look like someone who deserves to get paid. Can't afford a professional photographer? Here are some solutions.

Offer to trade or barter services with a professional photographer. Or, at the very least, surely the local college has a photography class. There will be a few advanced students who could take a proper headshot.

If we don't have anything now, at least do the best we can with our smartphone. Event planners need to see what we look like. Why? Are they prejudiced? No. But they do want to see if we look the part for the role they want us to fill. If we are guilty of poor dental hygiene, we won't be a good fit for the speech to second graders about the importance of brushing their teeth.

#2. Our topic or skill.

Event planners want experts who can speak, not speakers who claim they can fake their way through any topic.

It is better to focus on one topic or area. Experts get paid more. Experts are in high demand. Even if our only skill is being an emcee for events, we want to highlight that we are an expert in this area.

We will get more bookings when we focus. We will get fewer bookings if we claim to be everything to everybody. Make a business decision to focus on one area.

#3. Our demo video.

Nobody wants to book us if they haven't seen us perform. It is rare to get a "sight unseen" booking. Event planners want to see that we can deliver. Why? Because they want to keep their jobs.

We don't need a video of our entire talk. A two- or three-minute excerpt will be enough. If we don't have any video footage, now would be a good time to get some. Getting "live" video footage is best. It is hard to look good in front of an empty background pretending we are talking to an audience. Plus, if our video shows us talking in front of an audience, that is social proof that others book us.

We can get some video footage from previous speaking engagements. With a little bit of editing, we have our video. But what if we don't have previous speaking engagements?

Then, we will start with what we can do. If we have a budget, we can go to our local college and find a student in one of the media courses. Or perhaps, contact wedding videographers who are unemployed during the week. Maybe we can barter or trade for some quick footage.

If we plan for someone to make a video with their smartphone at our next speaking engagement, at least make sure we have good lighting.

#4. Our contact information.

Don't hide this in the fine print at the bottom of the page. We want people to contact us. Let the viewer of our website know that we look forward to visiting with them.

Ever get a business card where the email address is so small that it takes a magnifying glass to read? Few prospects will make the effort to do that. Make it easy for event planners to contact us. What should we include in our contact information?

Our name, phone number, and email address at the minimum. Also, including the city where we live may help event organizers who are looking for local speakers to keep travel costs within a tight budget.

Mark created a business card very early in his speaking career. It said Mark Davis, Speaker. He included his email and phone number, but no address because he was never there. But because he added "Speaker," people remembered him and what he did. It was simple, direct, and memorable. Oh, the card was bright red too. It stood out in the pile of white cards people collected at conferences and seminars.

Everything else on our webpage
can come later.

That beautiful full-color downloadable brochure, the creative capture box that leads to the sales funnel, the pages of glowing testimonials, and everything else can all be added later. For now, we have the minimum website needed to market our services.

Let's look at the organizer's point of view.

The event organizer wants to know what we speak about. Our website and demo video should answer that question.

Our demo video can help the event organizer determine if we would be a good fit for their audience.

Now all the event organizer has to ask us is:

#1. Are we available on this date?

#2. How much is our fee?

This makes the process easier and less stressful for the event organizer.

We won't have these two items on our site, our availability and our fees. This means we will have an actual conversation with the event organizer for these two items.

But can I start speaking before I create my website?

Yes. If someone asks, accept their offer.

We can get bookings from referrals, because of an association recommendation, or because we wrote a book or were in the news.

Bernie, Mark, and Tom all receive many bookings this way. But, it is better if we at least have a website. This makes it easier for event planners to contact us, and increases our bookings.

What about credentials?

Bernie has credentials. His training is approved for Continuing Professional Development (CPD) credits. Is this a plus?

Certainly. When proposing his training, he tells the organizer that all participants are eligible to receive CPD credits. That is a good selling point. That means the attendees don't have to attend an extra class that year to qualify for their points. And since they already want to come to Bernie's training class, they consider the CPD points an extra bonus incentive to attend.

So do you have to become a certified and approved instructor or coach before you begin your speaking career?

No. Many people become "certified" and never speak, coach, or train again. They don't know how to get bookings.

In Australia, Mark is certified to train many different professions. But once he travels overseas, which is often, none of these certifications matter.

And Tom? He is certified in nothing.

If you already have some certifications, great. Use them to add extra value. If you don't have any certifications, don't let that hold you back from a successful career.

Ultimately, people don't care about our certifications. They are more interested in our ability to solve their problems and make their lives better.

Now, back to more ways to get bookings. Because if you didn't get your calendar full from the first ideas, these will help you complete the task.

#4. The heavyweight champion of bookings.

A book.

Who can argue with an expert?

Instant credibility. We don't have to sell ourselves. It is uncomfortable to call someone up and say, "I am a really good speaker. I would like to speak at your event. Please hire me." Not exactly the best positioning.

If we've authored a book, our demo video becomes less important. Book authors are held in high esteem. Check out these statements for comparison.

- "I wrote a great blog article."
- "There is a video of me on YouTube."
- "I recorded an audio of me speaking."
- "Hey, check out this article I wrote for a magazine."

This doesn't do much for our credibility. Who would meeting organizers hire first? Someone who claims to be a good speaker, or someone who is an industry expert, an author of a book? Authors win almost every time. Yes, it is totally unfair. Sometimes reality is like that.

Meeting organizers want to feel that we bring great content and authority to their event.

Guess which introduction is more impressive to the audience?

#1. "Our next speaker is somebody who talks really well."

#2. "Our next speaker is the expert author of the book ..."

We can win awards, make audios, produce videos, collect testimonials, and even produce spectacular results for clients. However, nothing sells us more than having our own book.

Event planners and audiences want experts who can speak adequately, not great speakers with little actionable content.

But what about entertainment and performance? Yes, meeting organizers love that. They feel great when we perform well to their audience. But that is not what they originally asked for. They wanted content for their audience. If they only wanted entertainment, they could hire an actor or circus performer.

Is having a book better than someone with influence recommending us to others? Chances are we don't have someone with influence recommending us when we start. We are an unknown quantity. No one wants to risk their reputation on us.

But a book? That is something we can control. We can write our book, self-publish it, and be a superstar expert immediately. This is the heavyweight tool to move our speaking business forward.

We won't get rich from book sales, but we can get rich from the credibility of being a book author. We will get more bookings, and get paid more for these bookings as an author.

Remember Tom's story from the beginning of the book? He got invited to Hong Kong because a businessman saw his book and thought, "I want the author of this book to come speak to my salespeople."

And that was his first invitation to Hong Kong and China to speak. His speaking fee?

A trip to Hong Kong and China for Tom and his wife, with unlimited shopping for his wife. She took advantage of the shopping, so it was a fair trade of services.

- Did he have to sell the business owner on his services? No.
- Did he have to show a demo video? No.
- Did he have to produce references? No.

Because Tom was a book author, he received instant and full credibility. That is the power of a book.

So why don't more speakers, trainers, and coaches write a book?

Because it is hard.

Staring at a blank piece of paper or computer screen, trying to remember 8th grade English grammar, and trying to be a professional writer when we've trained ourselves in different careers is hard. Writing a book is hard even for professional writers!

But, dream for a moment. What if we authored a book for our industry? That would mean instant booking credibility. More speaking engagements. More workshops. Great training opportunities. And who wouldn't want to be coached by an expert who has even written a book? Plus, as the expert, our fees would be much higher.

Let's take a look at some of the reasons people wish they were the author of a book.

Why we want to be an author.

#1.   We have an ego. Everyone does. And it would be great to see our name on the cover of a book. We will look back at this years later, and feel like we accomplished something long-lasting. Being famous, even a little bit famous, feels good.

#2.   We have a message or skill deep within our hearts that we want to share with others. The book gives us an outlet for our passion.

#3.   A book builds our brand. It could position us as an expert in the industry. Any meeting organizer would love to have an expert of the industry talk to their audience. We don't have to prove our worth. All we have to do is give the meeting organizer our book. Done.

#4.   If we offer to autograph our book at the end of our speech, it gives the attendees a chance to meet us personally and connect. This could turn into extra revenue down the road.

#5.   Our book is the world's best business card. No one will throw it away. And if we exchange "business cards" with someone, they will be impressed.

#6.   Our book can be shared with others. We don't know who will see our book next. It might be a meeting organizer who thinks, "I want to book this person for our next event."

#7.   Our book means we can command larger speaking fees. It's hard to think of a better return on our investment.

#8.   Our book leads to well-paid consulting, training, and coaching events.

#9. If we promote our books to the right market, they will become a lead generation tool. For example, if our book was titled *64 Ways To Avoid Paying More Taxes*, who would we attract? Wealthier clients, of course.

#10. Our book could both educate people and sell our pro-duct or digital services. For example, if we sold the world's best skincare for acne, we could educate our audience not only in our talk, but also with our book. Our book could make even the most skeptical people want to try the product mentioned in our book.

#11. Our book could promote our events. One promoter sells his book to everyone at his free seminars, complete with two free tickets to his next event. At his next event, he upsells the atten-dees on his paid courses.

#12. Our book positions us to run our own event. We can then form our own group and network from a position of auth-ority and expertise.

Okay, we could fill a book about the benefits of a book. But the point is:

If we have a book, getting clients is so much easier.

Getting more clients, faster bookings, and more money to speak, train, or coach should be enough reasons to write a book. We will want to launch our book as soon as possible.

But we may be thinking, "I am not a writer!"

No problem.

Here is the good news. We don't personally have to write every sentence, work on grammar, or even do a coherent outline. This is what professional writers do for us. Authors are not necessarily the same people that do the writing and grammar-checking.

Now, if we are professional writers, of course, we should do it ourselves. But most speakers are not. They would rather spend their time speaking and promoting their career, instead of staring at a blank computer screen.

Get a professional writer started on your book now. It is the fastest and best way to launch one's career when starting out.

How much will it cost to get someone to help write our book?

The answer is, "It depends."

How long will our book be? Do we know what we want to say already? What do we want our book to accomplish? How soon do we need it? How much do we want to spend? Do we want to spend $10,000? $50,000? Should we have our neighbor's English-major daughter do it for tuition costs?

Good questions. Too many variables for this book, but here is a shorter suggestion.

Mark is an expert in this area and keeps up with the changing market. Email Mark at **CoachMarkDavis@gmail.com** and he can point you in the right direction in the current market.

But no matter what price range you decide on, or if you want to write the book yourself on weekends, remember:

"Every day we delay our book means money out of our pockets."

Just a simple increase in fees pays for the book quickly. Or, if we have trouble getting our first clients, our book will pay for itself immediately.

To get the biggest return from a book, concentrate on this mantra:

"Don't promote my book. Have my book promote me."

Never speak for free!

Don't. Just don't.

Cash-strapped organizations will ask us to speak for free. Some "negotiators" will want to see how cheaply they can hire us.

Professional speakers don't speak for free. This is what we do for a living.

Instead of thinking it is okay to speak for free, let us work out how to get paid every time.

(Okay, maybe one exception. If we speak badly, speaking for free could be overpayment for our services. But that is a problem for another book. For now, we assume everyone reading this book has public speaking skills, and wants to get paid for those skills.)

But what if our potential booking event has no cash or budget?

Cash isn't the only way to get paid. Let's broaden our options. Here are a few ways to not get paid in cash, but to still get paid in value.

#1. We need practice.

If we are new and need to practice our speech, consider our payment as renting their audience. It is better to practice our speech in front of "live" audiences. Then we can work on our timing, and see which parts of our speech create the best involvement. We can choose to practice in front of a mirror, or in front of an actual audience. Mirrors give poor feedback. Audiences give real-time valuable input to help us improve.

#2. We need exposure.

For example, we speak corporately. We could speak for free at their association event. We know there will be the right people in the audience who can hire us in the future.

This gives us a chance to advertise our services and leave a great impression. Consider this an audition.

Mark was the emcee for a 700-person conference in the Philippines. While having coffee, a delegate from Europe asked, "I know it's last-minute, but my friend has a company anniversary in Europe in five days. They need a keynote speaker. Are you available and what would it cost?"

That's the power of exposure. While the Philippine emcee speaking fee was modest, the European speaking fee was Mark's full rate. And it gets better. Because Mark could accommodate on short notice, the company appreciated this favor, and promised future bookings.

#3. Photo opportunity.

Will there be someone important from the company at the event? We can share the stage with them, and add that picture to our website for credibility.

If we have our picture with the Association's president, this will help us market to the other Association members. You and the CEO together in a photo creates a story for future marketing.

#4. Trade our speaking for introductions.

A charity might say, "We have no budget for a speaker." However, we know the charity has important people on their Board of Directors. The charity can offer to introduce us to their Board of Directors, and many of their local celebrity donors, in exchange for waiving our speaking fee.

We know these personal introductions will turn into future business. All we have to do is show up, speak, and meet these new people who will be grateful you spoke.

#5. The audience are "buyers."

Maybe we sell our book, coaching, consulting, or educational programs. If people in the audience are prospects, the sales revenue from our speaking event may be larger than an ordinary speaking fee.

Imagine we were speaking to a large group of 1,000 trainers. At the end of our speech, we offered a $300 continuing-education package. If only a small percentage of the 1,000 trainers purchased the package, this would exceed any normal speaking fee.

#6. Cover travel expenses.

If the organization cannot afford our speaking fee, they may offer to pay our travel expenses. If we have the possibility of other events in the area, this reduction in our travel expenses could make our other events more profitable.

When no cash is offered, it still does not mean "free." There are many ways we can receive value from our speaking that don't include cash. More ideas?

#7. Speak in exchange for our demo video.

If we are new and we don't have a demo video, this could be our chance. Propose this to the event organizer:

"If you can make a professional-looking video of my speech, I will waive my speaking fees. Provide me with a copy of the video for my use. And, you can have the right to use this video for training for your group."

From the video of our speech, we can take out excerpts, edit them, and have a five-minute demo video for our website. Now the only cost of our demo video is the cost of our editing.

#8. We want to be seen with famous people.

If we speak at an event with other famous people, like celebrities or sports stars, we may have a chance for a photo opportunity. And, if they heard us speak, we might even get a testimonial from them. Be prepared to record any interactions you have, and offer to include them in your future talks.

But enough reasons for now.

Let's get to an important question. "How much should I charge?"

How much should I charge?

Event planners have an agenda.

They want the best possible speaker for their event, at the lowest cost possible. They have an obligation to keep expenses low. That is their job.

We will get requests that say, "How much do you charge to speak?"

What can we reply?

We don't have any idea of their budget. If we quote too much, we won't speak. If we quote too little, that will cheapen our brand.

In this negotiation, who will quote a price first?

They might offer way more than what we would ask. Or, their first offer could be unacceptable.

Don't stress. Here is one way we can reply:

"I want to keep my speaking fees within your conference speaking budget if possible. What is the speaking and travel allowance for me to speak and train at your event?"

Some key points:

First, we said, "if possible." That means we are under no obligation to accept their first offer.

Second, if their first offer is low, we can find other ways to get more for our services. We could offer an extra breakout session or workshop while we are there. Or, offer something to sell to top off our revenue for the event.

Third, we mentioned "speaking" and "travel allowance." When we separate the cost into two categories, we typically will get more than having one price for everything.

Fourth, many times the event planner will offer more that we would have quoted. So by opening the conversation this way, we can get the best possible deal.

When possible, it is easier when we know the event's budget before quoting our services. Then we can factor in all our costs and ideal fees, and seem either exclusive or an absolute bargain.

But how much should we charge?

A variety of fees are possible.

Anywhere from $1 to tens of thousands of dollars per event.

Here are some considerations:

- What type of organization are we speaking to?
- What is their budget?
- What is our experience?
- Will our appearance help them sell more tickets?
- Can we sell products and services at the event?
- Who will be in attendance at the event?
- How much travel is involved to attend the event?

There are many more considerations, but we get the idea. We need to be flexible, especially in the beginning of our careers when we have few or no bookings.

When we become more famous, our presence at an event will help the event organizer sell tickets and appear more credible to the attendees. If our name helps promote the event, of course our fees will be higher.

After we are famous, everything is easier. But first, we have to build our public speaking career and reputation.

Whatever speaking fee we eventually quote, it is important to have a backup plan. We don't want to lose initial speaking events because we can't figure out how to make the finances work.

- If our transportation expenses are outside of their budget, could we try to get another event in the same area?

- Could we lower our fees for a multi-appearance commitment?

- Can the date of the speaking or training event be moved to a better time for us?

- Could we offer to do an additional special training to give them more value?

- Could we give a free online video class before the event that creates more value for the attendees? Or even help the event organizer promote the event?

With some forethought, we could suggest many options to make this a win-win for everyone.

And if there is no way we can get an in-person paid speaking event, as a last resort we can offer an online class or group webinar at reduced rates. If we can solve someone's problem, we need to try to develop a solution that works. After we get the first booking and deliver well, repeat business will be easy.

But this book is not about what fee to charge that is right for you. And it is not about your speaking skills.

Why? Because none of this matters if we can't get booked.

So, on to the next way to get bookings.

#5. Trusted non-speaker referrals.

Over 25 years ago, Mark was living in Melbourne. While working in the education industry, Mark made many contacts. One lady, Natalie, who worked for him briefly, moved on to work for an event management company. They organized the annual Australian International Furniture Fair among many other events.

This fair had exhibitors of furniture, lighting, accessories and wholesale ordering of items for hotels, restaurants and interior designers. They also provided paid workshops featuring famous designers, color specialists, and artists. Finally, they had free seminars on topics to assist the retailers, hoteliers, and restaurant owners. There were plenty of opportunities for speakers.

What did Mark know about furniture? Not much. All he had was some chair-sitting experience. But that is not what the organizer was looking for.

A few weeks before the event, Natalie's boss called Mark and said desperately, "We have no one to run the free seminars. Natalie suggested that I call you. We have seminars on retailing, selling, merchandising, and on the psychology of sales. And we have no one to run them. Our attendees look forward to these seminars."

Mark to the rescue. Mark did several 45-minute talks over the two-day event.

The best way to get future business? Do a great job today. People who see us perform can refer us to event planners. In this case, Natalie witnessed Mark's training when they worked together. It was easy for her to recommend Mark.

The furniture association was so happy that Mark saved the conference, they invited him back every year for six years.

This meant flights to Sydney, limousine transfers, five-star hotel accommodation, VIP access to welcome parties and private meetings, plus speaking fees and profits. But the initial $25,000 earned from these six annual events was only the beginning. Hundreds of businesses and entrepreneurs heard Mark teach about sales, marketing, and advertising. This led to more speaking opportunities and additional training workshops around the country.

Was Mark a furniture merchandising specialist? No. But someone else could cover that at the event. Mark taught the psychology of sales and advertising, giving the attendees more skills to take home.

Did Mark have any credentials or certifications on furniture merchandising? No. They didn't even ask about that when they called Mark to solve their seminar leader problem.

We don't need to limit our vision to one industry. Certainly we want to focus our marketing toward one industry, but let's be open-minded when others ask us to fill a need.

Let everyone know we are a professional speaker, trainer, or coach. We never know who they will come in contact with in the future. In this case, this one referral provided an instant booking with no questions asked. There was no speaker proposal, no committee to think it over. It was all done with one phone call.

That is the power of referrals, especially when they have an urgent problem to fix.

And remember, everyone in our audience could recommend or refer us in the future. Another example?

Mark was the emcee in Turkey for a corporate travel event. How did he get this event? From his translator at the original Hungarian event. His translator recommended that Mark could make their international event more interesting, and would relieve them of organizing the day's agenda.

In the audience of the event sat five Hungarian young men. They decided to start their own travel company. Once they had their company up and running, they arranged a huge conference in Antalya, Turkey for 1,300 people from 20 different countries. They needed an international speaker, a clear English-speaking native, as English would be the most common language at the event.

Here is what made this easy. First, Mark demonstrated and proved his ability to work with a translator. Second, Mark could travel. He would be in the Mediterranean on family holiday the week before the event anyway. With transportation and speaking fees, this made Mark's holiday free. In fact, more than free. By extending the holiday for a few days, he made a nice extra income.

The story doesn't end there. Six months later, the travel company approached Mark for consulting. They wanted to open operations in Asia. For the next six months they paid Mark consulting fees plus travel expenses. Sometimes our first talk is the advertisement for future work.

It is never about one speaking fee. Assume we will work with them again. This should motivate us to do the best job possible.

Be flexible.

We don't want to keep our speaking career a secret. Our personal friends should know exactly what we do. And if we can give them a quick one-sentence hook, they will remember this for the future.

Mark delivered a speech in Hungary, and was about to board a flight to the Netherlands. Before boarding his plane, he received a phone call from a friend. The organizer of an event in Bulgaria was desperate. His event started in two days. One of the main speakers had canceled because of illness. Could Mark be a substitute on two days' notice?

When Mark landed in the Netherlands an hour later, his friend messaged and said, "I checked. They definitely want you. Can you get on a quick flight to Bulgaria?" So Mark reclaimed his in-transit luggage and booked an immediate flight to Bulgaria.

Mark's friend, the Bulgarian event organizer, and the 800 delegates at the event all appreciated Mark's flexibility in changing his plans to deliver value for everyone attending. And for Mark? An additional speaking fee, all expenses paid, and even the sales of many books.

Many times, we have to be flexible. People will remember our generosity to them.

And a bonus for Mark for his quick change of travel plans? Glowing testimonials.

Getting testimonials.

Some people may not have the influence or power to book us. However, they can help our credibility by giving us positive testimonials. Here is Bernie's six-question formula to get quick testimonials from our coaching, trainings, and events.

Question #1: "Are you happy with the training?"

Question #2: "I am curious about what you liked best."

Question #3: "I am updating testimonials and thought of you."

Question #4: "Would it be okay if you could help me?"

Question #5: "I can show you some testimonials of others. Would that be okay?"

Question #6: "I could write it and have you approve it. Would that make it easier for you?"

As we can see, this makes it extremely easy for someone to give us a testimonial. Many times they are unsure about what to write. We take care of their objections with these easy questions.

You might think, "Is that all it takes to get testimonials? That is so simple and easy."

Exactly. Now, let's move on.

The best referrals?

When we do a good job, it is easy for others to refer us to their trusted contacts. They will feel confident that we will provide value, and they feel that there is no downside to recommending us. No one wants a bad recommendation to reflect on them and the referral.

This happens in a perfect world, sometimes.

But sometimes people are not pre-sold, and might be slightly skeptical.

After a particularly great speech, Bernie received some referrals. When following up with the referrals, he suffered from not having a strong relationship or connection. There was stress, and hesitancy to book him. Even with great recommendations, some companies are hesitant to invest money in a speaker or trainer.

Bernie's solution? For this particular insurance company, he would give the organizer great value and make the organizer look great. Here was Bernie's offer:

"Every one of the 100 attendees will get a $300 package of my audios and workbooks. But, you only pay $100 for each pack. Your company will get a great deal. And the attendees get it free. It is a great bonus because the company paid for it. They will love that they got more from this training than just words."

The event organizer agreed. This means Bernie received $10,000 for the 100 packs, instead of a $5,000 speaking fee.

Did the audience feel good towards Bernie? They felt great. They received tremendous value from Bernie's speech, and continuing value from the audios and workbooks they took home. At the end of his speech, many attendees approached Bernie and asked for personal coaching.

Another example of this technique?

A cash-strapped financial services event wanted Bernie to speak. It was close to Bernie's home, and Bernie had an opening that afternoon. Why not speak to build a relationship with the event organizer?

Bernie made the following offer: "I will drop by to speak at your event. And I will bring 60 books to give away to the attendees." Generous.

The event organizer replied, "But we have 200 people attending!"

Bernie: "Well then, you should buy 140 more books for them too." An instant sale of 140 books for Bernie.

Bernie delivered word-for-word scripts that the attendees could use immediately after leaving the conference. At the end of his talk, the line formed in the back of the room for Bernie. Everyone wanted their books personally autographed. Bernie chatted with them about coaching, audio programs, and additional training.

Mark uses this technique also. Here is an example.

Mark delivered a talk on storytelling techniques in Malaysia. Mark gave a free copy of his book on "Storytelling" to everyone in the audience. Throughout his talk, they could use the book to follow along with the different techniques.

At the end of Mark's talk, they saw that Mark had other books for sale in the back of the room. Mark sold out immediately.

Why does this work so well? First, if we do a good job, they want to know more. Second, we create a psychological debt by giving them something for free before we talk. And third, people appreciate our sincere desire to help them walk away with better skills for their lives.

If our connection to this referral is underwhelming, we must reach out and reduce the risk.

Networking events.

Networking socials, Chamber of Commerce events, meetup events and breakfasts. Sound familiar? Everyone does them.

How can we use these events for our business?

A simple change of focus will put us on the right path.

Here is the wrong way for us:

- Find big networking events.

- Pass out a lot of business cards.

- Ask others, "Do you need a speaker? A coach? More training?"

It isn't the quantity, it is the quality.

At networking events, we are better served by finding one or two high-quality connections. We will deepen these connections, possibly meeting them for lunch or coffee in the following days.

Our business will grow with quality connections, not by having hundreds of people with our business card in their desk drawers. Our goal is to build our network of quality connections.

Only quality connections will have the confidence in us, and enough influence with their connections, to produce solid referrals.

The larger our network, the better chance we have of positively answering this question:

"I would like to talk to the training director of the Big Company. Does anyone in my network know this person, or know someone at the Big Company that could connect me?"

This is the power of having a strong network of quality people.

Here is an easy way of keeping our focus on quality over quantity.

Replace the word "networking" with the word "connecting." Then, we will remember that it is the depth of the relationship that counts.

What do I say to organizers and prospects to get appointments and bookings?

What we say will be important.

How we say it is important.

What we offer is important.

Who we offer it to is going to be the most important!

So before we find great people to talk to, let's cover a few sales basics for when we do talk to a cold prospect. Basic human manners will apply.

> 1. The meeting organizer's time is valuable. They have other stuff to do. We need to get to the point now. Being asked a series of fact-finding questions is irritating for them. They don't have time to watch every speaker's demo video.

> 2. They want this conversation to finish quickly. They have fires to put out.

There are four main ways we will communicate with the organizers.

> 1. Email. Do we dread sending out endless unanswered emails to cold prospects? We should. It is the least effective way for us to get bookings. No one wants to spend their life chained to a desk, grinding out useless email requests.

2. Social media chat. Pretty impersonal, but better. The organizers can trace us to a social media profile and, if we have it already, our website. At least they can see what we look like.

3. Phone calls. Now we enter the world of two-way communication. They can ask questions and get answers immediately. One minute on the phone could replace a dozen back-and-forth direct messages or emails.

4. In person. Now we are rocking! The organizer can see our facial expressions, our body language, and we are not some cold-calling salesperson pitching over the phone.

No matter how we contact organizers, the following three steps help us keep the conversation short and moving forward.

Step #1. Ask permission. We might say, "Is now a good time to talk?" Basic manners.

Step #2. Ask a question or questions. With a very cold contact, we might feel only one question will be tolerated. If we don't feel stress from our listener, we could ask more questions. We must use good judgment. While our agenda is important, we want to be sensitive to our listener's comfort levels. What are some questions we could ask?

"When is your next event?"

"Where will you hold your next event?"

"What did the attendees like most at the last event or training?"

"How was your last speaker?"

"Which coaches have you worked with before?"

"Have you started planning your next event already?"

"What is the biggest hassle with organizing these types of events?"

Their answers will lead us to a comfortable transition to our next question. Keep it natural.

Step #3. Close quickly. No one wants our conversation to linger when they have other things to do.

Close? Yes.Okay, maybe we don't ask them to send us money now. But what do we mean by close?

We want to move this conversation forward. That could mean we agree to send them a demo video. Or a proposal. Or they will send us a schedule of their next training. We want to move forward with an action.

Afraid of making that initial call or contact? Don't worry. We are not asking for the sale now. We only ask that they make a decision to have a conversation with us. Remember, a decision to have a conversation is easier than a decision to buy.

We don't have to worry about giving a full PowerPoint presentation for them. Just ask a question. Our prospects will relax, feel the conversation is within their control, and continue a relaxed conversation with us. From this conversation we will learn if they have problems, any pressures they are under, and what they want.

Feel better? This is far simpler than the horror stories we can create in our minds.

As our prospects talk, they will tell us exactly what they are looking for, and tell us what objections they might have to our proposal. Here is an example.

Q. "How was your last speaker?"

A. "Oh it was terrible, the speaker billed $400 to the minibar and spoke nearly twice as long as we asked. Made our attendees stay overtime."

Q. "So you have a fixed budget for your next speaker?"

A. "Yes. $3,500 is our budget, and this time the speaker can pay for his own hotel and miscellaneous expenses."

Did we notice that the emotion from the event organizer was more about going over budget than about providing value to the attendees? We should make note of this.

If we know exactly what event organizers and prospects want, we will know how to make our services fit in better.

The three main questions.

Event organizers have to worry about production, event promotion, meeting room space, liability insurance, and more. When dealing with a potential speaker, the three most common questions are:

1. What do you speak about?

2. Are you available on this date?

3. What is your fee?

If we focus on answering these three questions, we will do fine as we start our career.

Can we improve over time? Sure. We will create better hooks for our talks, and better overviews. But for now, we have to get started.

And now, some more ways to get bookings.

#6. The emperor approach.

We run our own events.

Yes, we can be in charge of everything. We will create our own workshop or speaking event. As emperor of our speaking kingdom, we will control when and where we work. We don't have to wait for people to get back to us.

We will reframe our thinking this way:

"Instead of **getting** events, we will **create** events."

In the beginning, Bernie's diary was almost empty. So, he decided to create his own workshops. He targeted entrepreneurs and small businesses. He taught them ninja marketing techniques they could implement immediately.

Cost? Some events were free. Some had a nominal registration cost.

Marketing? Bernie promoted his workshops at the local networking events. For example, breakfast networking events, Chamber of Commerce events, etc. Bernie already had great phone skills, so he could also make cold phone calls to increase the attendance if needed.

At the end of the workshops, Bernie offered a service. The entrepreneurs could get coaching, a script, and a professional recording to put on their website. Two factors made this service irresistible.

First, it was inexpensive.

Second, Bernie did everything. He wrote the one- or two-minute script, coached the entrepreneur on delivery, and had his assistant record and edit the video. All the entrepreneur had to do was to show up for an hour. No preparation needed.

Now, let's ask ourselves, "As the entrepreneur's business grows, who will they want for coaching or further training?"

Bernie, of course.

No overhead, no risk.

Mark loves to teach public speaking skills. He says, "When we overcome our fear of public speaking, our confidence goes up. Everything we do gets better when we feel confident."

When Mark is at home in Australia, he has free or low-cost access to his condominium building's conference room. That means no cost or overhead for his local events. He only has to take the elevator downstairs.

With no overhead, how easy or profitable can it be to do our own events? We could almost pay people to come and still be profitable.

So instead of watching TV one evening, Mark can conduct a 3-hour workshop on "Overcoming the Fear of Public Speaking." When the attendees experience their fear disappearing in only three hours, they are impressed. At the very least, they buy a few of Mark's books. Some insist on high-priced personal coaching. And remember, every attendee knows who to recommend to their company for training and keynote speeches.

How did Mark fill his evening events?

1. He put announcements in the free local neighborhood paper.

2. He visited offices in the neighborhood.

3. He told others to promote the events and let their friends know.

4. He had his working friends tell him who is in charge of training at their jobs. Mark would call the appropriate person to invite their employees.

Everyone has a list.

From years of selling books across Australia, Mark created a list of self-improvement book buyers. While Mark had previously used other people's lists, this is an example of using his own in-house list.

When Mark received a paid speaking job anywhere in Australia, he would also run his own event the day after. His transportation expenses were already paid, so all he needed to do was find an inexpensive meeting room.

Mark did two different workshops at the time. One focused on overcoming the fear of public speaking, and the second workshop featured effective Google AdWords strategies. His personal list of book buyers usually filled his workshops. And if not, he did some Google ads or Facebook ads to help fill in the attendance.

If we don't have our own list, borrow the list of someone who has contacts in the area. Running our own personal workshops can be highly profitable, especially if all our travel expenses are already paid.

Professional introducers' events.

Bernie invented this.

Think small.

Bernie works with financial advisors. They would like quality referrals instead of prospecting and making cold calls. A quality referral for them means that a business professional pre-sold a current client to do business with them. It is not only a strong referral, it is an endorsement.

Financial advisors can earn huge fees working with retirement accounts and pensions. Each good referral could mean thousands in fees. But don't limit your vision only to financial advisors. This works for accountants, the legal profession, and more.

Bernie helps the financial advisor invite accountants, lawyers, funeral home directors, and influencers to the networking event. The invitation is easy. The financial advisor might invite his personal contacts by saying, "I want to give you access to my personal network. Come to this three-hour event, learn new skills, and meet my personal network. This will be a good way for you to expand your business also."

The financial advisor host is not qualified as a public speaker, so Bernie teaches and entertains the group of 12 to 15 attendees for three hours. Because Bernie is qualified, he can also give them CPD credits if they need them for their profession. Being CPD-qualified is not a necessity, but it is a nice benefit that Bernie offers.

The attendees make new contacts and learn new skills. The host creates a strong bond with these attendees. The host will meet with them one-on-one later for coffee or lunch to further that relationship. From these coffees and lunches, they understand each other's businesses better, and the attendees start sending pre-sold people to the financial advisor.

But it doesn't end there.

They arrange another networking event for the group in two months' time. Each attendee is asked to bring a friend to the second event. Again Bernie's services are needed to teach and entertain.

How does Bernie find financial advisors that want to do these events? He says this:

> "There are two types of financial advisors in the world.

> "Those that spend their careers making cold calls, prospecting strangers, attending time-wasting networking events, and begging contacts for low-quality prospects. They lose valuable time in their careers.

> "And those that spend their working time with the right high-quality prospects. They get a steady stream of pre-sold prospects sent to them by their private network of professional introducers."

They pay Bernie a lot of money for each three-hour speaking appearance.

Bernie can create these events on-demand.

#7. The grow approach.

Remember this from earlier in this book?

"Instead of **getting** events, we will **create** events."

Now, we will change a few words.

"Instead of **getting** clients, we will **grow** new clients."

Starting now, we can begin growing our contact list of loyal clients. How will we do this?

1. Target the exact type of client we want. Will this client be able to pay our speaking fees? Do our skills bring great value to this type of client?

2. Begin creating a relationship with these clients. Reach out to them and be incredibly helpful. Volunteer suggestions on what they could do better. Help them find overlooked niches. Refer potential customers to them. Pass on industry news they may not know about.

3. It is easier to get an appointment about our training and coaching services once we have a relationship.

4. And many times we don't have to pitch what we offer. They already know. They can reach out to us when they need us. We can hurry this along a bit by passing on a few appropriate testimonials.

As a longtime company owner, Tom had competitors. Every industry has competitors.

Competitors meet at Association events. Surprise, surprise. Everyone is friendly at these events. Yes, we are competitors, but we all face the same challenges in our industry. If someone had the same challenge that Tom faced, he shared what happened to his company and how he solved it.

Guess what? One competitor appreciated the help so much, he invited Tom as a speaker for one of their big events. And then another. And then another. And soon, many competitors asked Tom to speak. As a general rule, it pays to help everyone, even our competitors. As they grow, they will continue to need help.

Think of businesses. Most are understaffed and struggle to survive. Government regulations, cash flow, market conditions, and everyday challenges make it hard to stay in business. When we reach out and volunteer even the tiniest bit of help, they remember. Now we are building rapport with people we can talk to about our speaking, training, or coaching services.

Attempting to cold-call companies seldom works. Sending an email is even more impersonal. And if we start the email with "To whom it may concern," don't even send the email.

Yes, we could get clients by cold-calling every day, but do we want to make hundreds or thousands of cold calls? That is not a speaking career. That is a telemarketing sales career.

If you have great cold-calling telephone skills, and you love to do it, then by all means continue. You are a rare individual. But most of us would rather be speaking instead of cold-calling every day.

Here is a list of ten things we can do to create new relationships as we grow potential clients:

1. Recommend a potential employee for them to interview that would be great for a job opening they posted.

2. Let them know about a tradeshow or an opportunity for them to showcase their business.

3. Forward an article that may be important for one of their departments.

4. Let them know about any tax incentive programs announced for their area.

5. Offer a great headline or better copy for one of their brochures.

6. Let them know about a low-cost vendor for something they are purchasing now.

7. Recommend a service or program that we've used successfully.

8. Let them know how they can get inexpensive interns from the local university.

9. Tell them about a great restaurant that will save them money on their employee Christmas party.

10. Refer a potential client to one of their salespeople. If a sale is made, the salesperson will be more than happy to sing our praises to anyone in their company.

Ten only? No. This is only a start. With a little imagination we can do much better.

When we reach out to help people, they remember.

In the beginning of our careers, we may not have a giant list of happy clients. We might not have any prospects at all. And even if we do not get our first speaking events quickly, growing our own clients is something we can start doing immediately.

We don't want to waste time in our careers. Investing time into growing clients pays off. Whenever we feel that we have nothing productive to do, let's grow more clients.

Executive coaching.

Bernie knows marketing. And he is not shy about volunteering to help someone in need. He does this with no expectation of return favors. Being a nice person pays off.

Some of his small coaching clients grew into big clients. As they moved up in their careers, so did their power and influence.

Now Bernie coaches top executives and famous athletes in England on presentation and delivery skills. This gives him fame and status and makes each new booking easier. While high-paid executive coaching pays well, the bookings pay better.

Executives want to be coached by the best. And the best, in their minds, is anyone who is recommended by peers they respect. So to get better clients, make sure your best clients connect you to their networks.

#8. Podcasts.

With hundreds of thousands of podcasts to choose from, we can find plenty for our niche. Yes, there are podcasts from everything from knitting to astrology. And people love podcasts. That is why it is one of the fastest-growing industries today.

Imagine someone has a podcast. Every week that person needs a new guest. We could be that guest. Podcasts need a fresh inventory of interesting guests forever. They don't want to keep interviewing the same people over and over.

As a professional coach, speaker, or trainer, we have the ability to be an interesting guest. They don't want someone who is shy, can't put thoughts together, and won't have a good message for their listeners.

Getting on a podcast isn't hard. Think about what the podcast host wants. The host wants interesting topics to entertain the listeners. All we have to do is locate the podcasts we want to be on, then offer them a fantastic interview. Whether we contact the podcast team by email or phone, we want to prepare an interesting "hook." Then, have a quick two- or three-sentence benefit statement. That's it.

Podcast hosts get lots of requests. They don't have time to listen to long sales pitches, yet almost everyone gives them one. We will stand out by having our short benefit statement ready for them.

An example of a good hook or benefit statement?

Imagine we talk to a health podcast host. Our hook?

"I will ask your audience this question: 'What is a common first symptom of heart disease?' While the audience thinks, I will answer it for them. 'Instant death!' Then, I will go through the next four most common symptoms. It will be a break from listening to boring speakers quoting data from recent research reports."

Done. We are the speaker. We are the expert. This is not hard.

Our podcast interview has many benefits. First, we can get the recording and post it on our website. This would give a potential meeting organizer a chance to review how we perform and sound. Remember, they want to make sure we're good before they hire us.

Second, when people subscribe to a podcast, they normally listen to many of the past episodes. That means our interview will be heard over and over for months and years to come.

Third, we can practice our material in this podcast. We can listen later to see how we could have done better.

Fourth, we can practice our material to an audience that is giving us zero "live" feedback. Most podcasts are pre-recorded. This is important because our next speech could be to a very difficult audience. We will want to notice how fast we talk when we have no audience feedback. The natural tendency is to speak faster. Here is a good chance for us to test ourselves.

Fifth, if we are good on one podcast, other podcasters want us. There is a close community of podcasters in every niche.

And did we notice?

We didn't have to start our own podcast. That is a lot of work and a huge commitment of time. We would only do this if we had a huge passion for our topic that could be could sustained over many years.

#9. Stalking.

Some speakers have all the luck. Huge speaking fees, yet limited talent. (Okay, our egos will always say other speakers offer less value than we do. This is called, "Human nature.")

Mark did something about this.

Mark followed one of these overpaid speakers on Facebook. The speaker posted videos of his successful events in front of large audiences. One of this speaker's events was in a country Mark wanted to visit. It didn't take much investigation to discover the name of the event and the event organizer.

Mark reached out. He offered help and resources to the organizer.

Resources?

It takes no time for us to send an organizer a note like this:

"I know you are in the management training industry, and I came across this article that may be useful in your upcoming newsletter." Or we can find an ebook, video, website, cartoon, or report that benefits the organizer.

But back to the stalking.

Over a period of three months, a great relationship developed. Mark even offered to locate other speakers and negotiate their terms for the organizer's next big event. This was easy to do. Mark had a large speaker's network and good relationships with those speakers.

The organizer did not have contacts with other international speakers. This saved the organizer time reviewing, contacting, and negotiating with unknown speakers.

The organizer was so grateful, he included Mark among the speakers for the next big event. And yes, Mark received a huge speaker's fee. But not just once. He got paid over and over again for many of this organizer's events.

When the organizer realized Mark had authored five books, he offered Mark five licensing fees to be the exclusive publisher of his books in his country. With over 10,000 books sold in the country, this was a win-win arrangement. The organizer became one of Mark's closest friends.

If we are not getting huge speaking fees, someone else is. That someone could be us. All we have to do is find the event organizer that pays huge speaking fees, and make sure we get in line. Often the speaker who gets the big fee only gets it once. Either the budget is gone, or the organizers don't get the profitable return they expected. So they politely delay that speaker's return, and look for other alternatives.

Let's ask ourselves, "Who pays well in my industry?" Then, let's find out when their next event, training, or coaching session will be. Finally, build a helpful relationship with the organizer. We have many talents, resources, and skills we can use to help the organizer. And yes, it may start with something as small as sharing an article about spreadsheet planning.

The highly-paid speakers will not even notice that we stalked them and developed new business for ourselves. They are too busy accepting their next high-paying gig. They wouldn't get re-booked anyway. Organizers are always looking for fresh, new speakers for their next event.

Find five speakers like this, and we can start booking high-paying speaking opportunities.

Preparing our signature hook.

A hook is a short sentence or phrase that draws people in and makes us interesting. On the Internet, we see hooks all the time. Most times they are click-bait. These are ugly spam sentences that hope to draw us into going to their page. Click-bait articles have headlines such as:

"Elvis' two-headed baby marries space alien."

"The one thing you should never do to your face."

"You won't believe what this movie star looks like now, 30 years later."

Newspapers use hooks. They call them headlines. If we don't like the headline, we will not read further.

If we pay for advertising, we want a good hook to draw in customers.

The subject lines and first sentences of our emails are excellent places for a good hook to get prospects to continue reading.

With short attention spans, our market barely has time to listen to our first sentence. That is why it is important to create a powerful hook to get people to book us.

Why? Consider this conversation.

Prospect: "So what do you do for a living?"

Us: "I am a speaker."

Prospect: "Well, what do you speak about?"

Us: "Uh, uh, well, it is sort of an inspirational speech for people who want to feel better about the negative experiences in their lives …"

This will not end well.

We need an awesome hook that gets our listener to say, "Wow. That would be perfect for our group. Please come and speak to us."

Our hook can be about our brand, our unique message, or something that identifies us and makes us memorable.

But the best hooks are benefit-filled statements that solve a problem. We want our prospect to nod, agree, and want to continue.

After our hook, it would be great if our prospect thought:

"That is something I need now."

"I didn't know that. Tell me more."

"Wow! That could solve my problem."

"This is exactly what our event needs."

Our hooks should be memorable. So to get more business, let's put some hooks in our sentences to attract bookings. Here are some examples of hooks for different speeches.

"Lazy employees? I fix that."

"Office not working as a team? I show them how."

"Salespeople depressed in today's market? I will rejuvenate them."

"Students won't plan and set goals? I make it fun for them to do so."

"I get donors excited about your charity project."

"I make sure your meetings run smoothly, and you will never be embarrassed as the organizer."

"I turn dieters into normal people."

"I create super-negotiators in 45 minutes."

Yes, this book is about getting more bookings. Getting in front of the right people is very important. But let's not forget that once we are in front of the right people, we will have to say something. Many people prejudge us based upon the first few words out of our mouths.

They bombed the airport!

As Bernie gets off his flight into Turkey to change planes, a bomb explodes. Bernie looks around to see if everyone is okay. There is dust everywhere.

After a few minutes of chaos, people are told to sit and wait while things get sorted out. Bernie sits next to a man and starts a conversation. This man has a friend who is a CEO of a company. This is a perfect time for a "hook" or a benefit statement of what we can provide to others. People need to pass our message along.

After listening for potential problems, Bernie told his new friend this: "I help businesses get more appointments without even selling."

Bernie's new friend recommended that Bernie speak to his CEO friend. And, Bernie got the booking.

Having a well-prepared hook that solves problems is half of the solution. We have to remember that the first half of the solution is to listen for a problem that we can solve.

A great hook gets people to want to listen more.

A great hook can go viral and get us more exposure.

A great hook can help build our brand.

This is not a book about copywriting, but think like a copywriter. What could we say that is so irresistible that the listener wants to hear more?

#10. Social media?

Go to LinkedIn. Search for speakers. Then search for trainers. Then search for coaches.

Okay. We get the point. Everybody wants to be a speaker, trainer, or coach. It is too hard to stand out if we only market ourselves in one place. We don't want to starve.

Now, this does not mean we should not be on LinkedIn if we want to be a professional speaker. This only means we shouldn't depend on LinkedIn for all of our marketing. Some organizers will look for us on LinkedIn to do their due diligence on our qualifications. That makes sense.

But should we spend hours marketing our LinkedIn page? Take $500 courses on how to stand out on LinkedIn? Probably not. As we can see from the previous ways of getting bookings, we want to put our time into the booking methods that get results quickly.

But, can it happen? Could we actually get a booking from our LinkedIn account?

Yes, and when it does, we should accept it as a gift.

An example?

Mark created his LinkedIn account in 2006 and updates it like a living resume. Keeping the account relevant and accurate is important. Here is why.

A hotel company from India scheduled a manager training retreat in Bangkok, Thailand. If top management did all the training, they would put the attendees into a coma. They needed a fresh, outside speaker about manager-employee relationships. Guess who lived in Bangkok at the time? Mark.

They probably searched LinkedIn for English-speaking speakers who live in Bangkok. This keeps their retreat expenses within their budget.

As luck would have it, Mark could walk to the venue from his condo. All they had to pay was his speaking fee.

Now, what if Mark had not updated his profile? His profile would have shown that he lived in Australia. And that means no call for this event. And what about future business from this event? This is a fast-growing hotel company, with 2,000 employees. There are plenty of future speaking and training opportunities.

Should we depend on social media for bookings? No. But if one comes in, accept it with a smile.

#11. Be first.

In 2006, Mark and Tom climbed Uluru, the giant red rock in the middle of nowhere, Australia. Not much to do in the Australian Outback, so they had plenty of time to think and plan.

Mark discovered Google AdWords to be an exciting way for businesses to advertise for customers. Now, Google AdWords was six years old at this time. It took a while for them to develop the market, but it was too complicated for a small business to manage. Most small businesses couldn't handle it, and they couldn't afford expensive consultants to do it for them. Mark saw a market.

Mark said, "I am going to speak about Google AdWords. I will train small businesses on how to do basic ads for themselves." Yes, there were a few other experts, but definitely not enough experts to go around. This was a brand-new industry.

After a week of intensive study to upgrade his AdWords skills, Mark was ready. An expert is someone who knows more than everyone else in the room.

The market was easy. Mark could fill his workshops with some targeted Google ads in any city he wanted to visit. When the thirst for knowledge is there, marketing is easy. Over the next two years Mark branded himself as "Google Superman," while becoming even more of an expert in this area.

What happened next? It got boring. If we don't enjoy what we teach, train, or coach, we have the freedom to move on. That is what Mark did. This is great news for everyone reading this book. We will never feel bored. We can create an interesting speaking career by learning a new subject that we feel excited about.

If we are first-to-market with new information that people want, event organizers would love to feature us at their events.

How do I promote this?

If our message or information is new, then most likely no one knows about it. Our topic may have never crossed their minds. So how do we get exposure? How do we approach casual networking contacts with what we do?

The solution is easy, especially if we have a passion for our topic.

Do a weekly conference call or webinar. Make it free for people to attend.

Here we can talk about our topic, answer questions, and introduce people to the "authority" ... which, of course, is us.

We don't have to worry if only meeting organizers or managers listen. Anyone listening could recommend us for their event. Or, anyone listening might become a private coaching client.

When we do this to educate our market, it might be all the brand marketing we need.

Some bad ideas.

Okay, maybe not bad ideas, but ideas that will certainly yield low returns on our time investment.

Q. What about getting registered with a Speaker Bureau?

In the beginning of our careers, this probably won't work. Speaker Bureaus are for speakers who already have a demand for their services. If we are looking for someone to hire us, these bureaus won't be interested. They want famous, in-demand speakers. We don't qualify.

Even if we submit the perfect one-page document, complete testimonials, and other requirements, the agencies won't want us because we are not already in demand. Their job is to negotiate contracts with companies and fill their needs with proven talent, not to ask meeting organizers to risk a new speaker at their event.

Instead of trying the near-impossible, let's invest our time into one of the many other techniques in this book to get more bookings.

Q. What about sitting at home for weeks sending cold emails to event organizers?

Slow, tedious, and a very low chance of success. How would **we** respond to emails from strangers? And now, as a stranger, we are asking people for money to speak? Ugh!

There is nothing wrong with this technique, but it may not be enough for us to kick-start our career. And sending out cold emails? Is that the activity we envisioned in our career?

Q. What about hiring a social media marketing firm and getting some public relations help? Hire someone to spend days on social media, video streams, and posting motivational quotes on our many channels?

We might go hungry. There are tens of millions of photos posted every day. Without a targeted market viewing them, these photos go into the void of cyberspace. Only our mother, worthless brother-in-law, and a few bored teenagers will give us "likes" and "views" in the beginning.

We will build our following organically by performing our best at our talks.

So does this mean we should never post on social media? Of course not. But rather than random, unplanned posts, let's make a few quality posts instead. Then, let's get on with working to get more bookings.

#12. Be awesome.

As we know, the best way to get new bookings is for someone to see our awesome performance at any event. That is a good reason to always do our best.

When we finish our awesome performance, let's make it easy for others to contact us. Stay behind. Talk to the audience. Make new contacts.

And when we don't have bookings, now is a good time to plant seeds for future bookings. Build stronger relationships. And of course, work on improving our speeches, trainings, and coaching.

There should be no wasted time in our business. We are either planting seeds for new business, or reaping the harvest from the seeds we've already sown.

This isn't the book for improving our talks. But the old adage about starting strong and ending strong will always apply.

In the beginning of our careers, we might do a bit of subtle promotion in our talks. For example, we could mention how we've helped other people or organizations with a problem. We want to plant a seed in the audiences' minds, so if they ever need a speaker, they will think of us. Later, once we have our careers going, we won't need to do this.

But nothing sells more than a spectacular talk that changes how the audience feels. That should always be our #1 promotional tool.

What to do when we don't have bookings.

It happens.

After the panic subsides, what should we do? Where do we start? How do we start? Who should we speak to first?

Here is Bernie's #1 piece of advice.

Go back to our previous clients. Yes, they don't want to book us again. They've already heard us. And their audience wants to hear someone new. But what if it didn't cost anything?

During a quiet period, Bernie called some of his previous clients. He made this offer: "I would like to help even more. I can do a 30-minute follow-up webinar to help them remember the skills they learned. I am happy to do it for them at no cost."

The client was happy. The webinar attendees were thrilled. They enjoyed the extra value.

What happened? You guessed it. More business, new coaching clients, and more bookings. We never know when it is the right time for our clients to need us again.

Bernie's second piece of advice?

Mend our nets!

Bernie asked a successful restaurant owner, "How did you get started in the restaurant business?" And the restaurant owner told this story.

"I started out as a young man working on a fishing boat. Unskilled as a fisherman, I bounced from boat to boat trying to make a living.

"Over the years I noticed most nets had holes in them, so we lost some fish in every catch. And when the seas got too rough to fish, the boats stayed closer to shore and caught fewer fish. Sometimes the boats had engine problems and we experienced 'downtimes' during repairs. Plus, many crews got drunk in the local pubs during repair time. As a result of these problems, a lot of time and money was lost.

"Eventually I saved enough money to buy my own boat. Now I knew how to work more efficiently than the other crews.

"When the weather got bad and the seas were too rough, I used my 'downtime' wisely.

"I mended my nets. Worked on the engine. My competition complained about downtime at the local pub.

"When the weather cleared, I went back to the sea. No more leaky nets, and my engine didn't let me down.

"What did my competition do when the weather cleared? They started repairing and mending their nets, while I was already out at sea bringing in a huge catch!

"I learned that when I could not go to work because of challenging circumstances, that was the best time of all to mend my nets and prepare myself for when I could go back to work!

"That simple idea kept me profitable, very profitable! In time, I purchased more boats, and then this restaurant.

"Storms and rough seas do not last forever. Eventually things turn around, and when they do, I want to be ready to expand my business!"

He had discovered the secret to any industry: "Don't waste our downtime. Mend our nets!"

We can always practice our talk.

We can always write more material.

We can always prepare more stories.

We can always ask for more referrals and testimonials.

We can always deepen our relationships.

Even when we are not on the stage, we can do many things to further our careers.

A few final resources.

In the beginning of this book, we mentioned that getting bookings is not the only skill we will want in our career. Here are a few resources in those other areas we will want to excel in.

Mark and Tom wrote a book several years ago called *Public Speaking Magic: Success and Confidence in the First 20 Seconds.* If we want to get the audience on our side immediately, this is a great book (from our biased viewpoint).

If you want to know more about Mark's books and services, you can visit his website at:

markdavis.com.au

Bernie and Tom wrote a book called *Getting "Yes" Decisions: What insurance agents and financial advisors can say to clients.* If you want to master the words and phrases that will convert potential clients to lifelong clients, this is the book for you.

You can check out Bernie's coaching services, blog, events, and more at his website:

berniedesouza.com

Tom wrote a book called *Create Influence: 10 Ways to Impress and Guide Others.* Influence gives us the power to affect others and our world. Having influence will be a driving force behind our public speaking careers.

You can check out Tom's website at:

bigalbooks.com

For the big picture on public speaking careers, Grant Baldwin has an excellent free podcast called *The Speaker Lab*. Enjoy hours and hours of great episodes.

You can learn to overcome your fear of public speaking with a Dale Carnegie course. Many people also learn their skills with Toastmaster. Both organizations are everywhere.

A quick search on Google for "how to be a great coach" brings up 945 million matches. And a search for "how to be a great trainer" brings up 664 million matches. That should be enough for anyone to start.

Resources are nice, but action is what counts.

Good luck filling your personal calendars with bookings.

—Bernie, Mark, and Tom

Thank you.

Thank you for purchasing and reading this book. We hope you found some ideas that will work for you.

Before you go, would it be okay if we asked a small favor? Would you take just one minute and leave a sentence or two reviewing this book online? Your review can help others choose what they will read next. It would be greatly appreciated by many fellow readers.

More books from
Fortune Network Publishing:

bigalbooks.com